Music To
Make Friends By
By Hayley Long

Published by Rily Publications Ltd 2019
ISBN 978-1-84967-4072
Copyright © Hayley Long 2019

The Quick Reads project in Wales is an initiative coordinated by the
Welsh Books Council and supported by the Welsh Government.

Printed and bound by CPI Group (UK) Ltd, Croydon, CR0 4YY
Cover design by Welsh Books Council

CYNGOR LLYFRAU CYMRU
WELSH BOOKS COUNCIL

Noddir gan
Lywodraeth Cymru
Sponsored by
Welsh Government

Music To Make Friends By

By Hayley Long

This book is full of things that really happened.
To make up for any gaps in my memory, I
may have added a few extra details too.
And once or twice I've changed a name.
But trust me – I'm a storyteller.

Chapters

CHAPTER ONE
Big Questions

'Urggh! How can you listen to this?'

It was *that* question again! Even though I was forty-six years old, I suddenly felt like I was fifteen. Fighting back an urge to giggle, I took one hand off the steering wheel and turned up the volume on my car stereo.

'You've turned it up,' said my mum, who was in the seat next to me. 'I just said I don't like it!'

'Yes, but *I* do,' I said. 'And we're in my car.' I risked a quick glance sideways. My mum had pressed her lips together and was frowning. To be fair, it wasn't exactly feel-good music that was spilling out of the speakers. A very gloomy woman was muttering along to a guitar. Her song was called 'When Were You Happy?'

A few more seconds passed and then my mum said, 'Who is this then?'

'Laura Marling,' I said, cheerfully. 'She's an English folk singer. I think she's a genius.'

In the corner of my eye, I saw my mum shake her head and pull a face. A few more seconds passed and then she said, 'I don't.'

On a reflex, I reached out and nudged the volume up

a bit more. It was childish, I know, but the devil had got into me. Straightaway, Laura Marling started muttering a bit louder and I started to laugh.

My mum waggled her finger at the dashboard. 'I don't think she's as good as Ed Sheeran. No way! It's no wonder I've never heard of her.'

I stopped laughing.

'Ed Sheeran is so popular,' said my mum. 'I was in a supermarket the other day and his song about the castle on the hill was playing and everyone was tapping the tune on their trollies and singing along.' A smile crept into her voice. 'He appeals to *everyone*.'

I felt my stomach sink. We'd had this conversation before. And I knew *exactly* what question was coming next.

'So why don't *you* like him?'

I gripped the steering wheel a little tighter and said, 'When have I ever said that I don't?'

'I think he's very talented,' said my mum. 'Don't you think he's talented?'

'Yes, of course I do!'

'So why ...? My mum's voice drifted into a sigh.

This was terrible! I turned the stereo off and tried to think of something helpful to say but my mind had gone completely blank. *What was wrong with me? I love* music. I love pop, rock, jazz and disco. I love hip-hop, soul and funk. I even own a copy of *The Muppet Show Album*. When it comes to music, I have *very* broad taste. So why couldn't I chat to my mum about Ed Sheeran?

Taking my eyes off the road, I risked another quick glance sideways. 'Music is ... personal, isn't it?'

My mum shrugged. Then, with the wisest words in the world, she knocked this tricky topic on its head and cleared the air. 'It's a good job we're all different,' she said. 'Wouldn't it be boring otherwise?'

After that, we chatted happily about other things and the stereo stayed off. But my stereo never stays off for long. As soon as I was alone again, I switched it back on. This time, the song that my MP3 player chose was 'Stutter' by a nineties band called Elastica. It was a punky riot of noise complete with squealing feedback and crunching guitars. I let out a laugh. My mum wouldn't like this song either!

But then I remembered what she'd said about Ed Sheeran and frowned. He appeals to everyone. Or *nearly* everyone. A lot of the music that I love is like Marmite. People either love it or hate it. I drove the rest of the way home thinking about that.

I'm still thinking about it now.

What does any of it mean?

And why do I love the music that I do?

CHAPTER TWO
Kid Rock

I have always loved music. When I was six, I was given a bright orange keyboard for Christmas and I was so excited that I was nearly sick. With this wonderful piece of kit, I was going to transform myself into a famous keyboard player, just like Benny from Abba or Dr. Teeth from The Muppet Show Band. I couldn't wait to get started.

Sadly, my mum and dad forgot to buy any batteries so I spent the whole of Christmas Day playing with my brother's Action Man instead.

On Boxing Day, I asked my parents to go to the shops and get some batteries but they told me that everywhere would be shut and I'd have to wait another day. The keyboard stayed in its box.

The next day, my batteries arrived and, at last, I was ready to make sweet music. Wasting no time, I switched the keyboard on. A strange whirring noise began to groan out of it. It sounded as if there were a gust of wind trapped inside. A little worried, I pressed down on one of the chunky white keys. After a slight delay, a very thin beep wheezed out.

I tried a black key. A split second later, I heard another

beep which was just as weak and wheezy as the one before but slightly higher in pitch.

Moving my hand to the other end of the keyboard, I tried one of the keys there. It made a noise like the sad squeak of a sick hamster.

I started to feel upset. Maybe I wasn't doing it right? I tried another approach and pushed the palms of both my hands down on as many keys as I could. This time, no notes came out at all. There was only that strange groaning wind. After a few more attempts, I switched the thing off. I'm not sure if I ever played with it again.

I was only six years old but that Christmas of 1977 taught me something important. To make music, you need lots of patience and a half-decent instrument. I had neither. It seemed easier to leave this difficult task to the people on *Top of the Pops*. From now on, I was just going to *listen* to music instead.

Even though my keyboard was unloved and untouched, there was always plenty of music in our house. When I was very little, songs were stacked up next to the record player in the form of seven-inch singles. These black vinyl discs lived inside square paper sleeves and came from shops like Woolworths, Debenhams and even Boots the Chemist. They cost about 50p each. As soon as the single started spinning on the turntable, some sort of wonderful magic happened. That black vinyl circle was turned into sound!

Most of the singles in our house belonged to my mum. She played them over and over again and I spent the 1970s singing along to every word. Back then, my favourite singles were 'When I Need You' by Leo Sayer and 'Beautiful Lover' by Brotherhood of Man. My mum and I were also big fans of an American girl rocker called Suzi Quatro. Suzi wore a leather catsuit and played an electric guitar. I thought she was the coolest woman in the world.

At nine years old, I discovered the coolest *man* in the world. Or so I thought! He was a rocker, too, but instead of leather, he wore a scruffy denim jacket and matching scruffy jeans. This snarling bad boy had oily hair and twitchy feet and I loved him so much that I begged my mum to take me to the shops so I could buy his single. Little did I know it, but this trip into town was to be an important milestone. It would provide me with the answer to a very important and personal question:

What was the first record you ever bought?

I wish now that I could say it was something by Blondie or Davie Bowie or Adam and the Ants. If I ever *have* said that

I was lying. The truth is actually a little less hip.

One day in 1981, my mum took me into Woolworths in Ipswich. We made our way past the Pick 'n' Mix sweets and the Harvest Café and followed the sound of music to the record department. Even though we were still in the same store, it suddenly felt a little different. The lights were dimmer, the music was much louder, and behind a long counter, a young woman with scary make-up and spiky hair was serving customers while she danced.

My mum pushed me forwards and said, 'It's your record – you should ask for it.' Perhaps my mum was embarrassed by the record that I was about to buy?

I waited nervously in the queue. When it was my turn to be served, I looked up at the dancing punk and said the words which were going to stay with me forever. 'Can I have "This Old House" by Shakin' Stevens please?'

The punk stopped dancing and shook her head. 'No, no, no,' she said. 'It's an *ole* house! Shaky is too cool to say the D.'

I stared at her in terror. Did this mean I could have my record or not?

The punk wiggled her shoulders and started dancing again. 'One second,' she said, and then spun around and started running her finger from left to right along the shelves behind her. I stood on tip-toes to watch. The shelves climbed from floor to ceiling and each one was crammed full with little vinyl records tucked inside plain cardboard sleeves. I'd never seen so many singles in my life! There were hundreds of them and they were packed together so tightly that you couldn't have slipped a postcard between them. A moment later, the punk found what she was looking for and pulled one of the cardboard pockets free. Then she slid out the record and put it inside a nicer sleeve which had a picture of my hero on the front.

'There you go,' she said, handing me a paper bag with my single inside it. 'The Welsh Elvis is all yours.'

With my heart thumping against my ribs, I handed over my money.

'Enjoy,' said the punk, and then she winked.

I walked back to my mum with the precious package in my hands. It felt good. It felt solid. It actually felt a little bit heavier than I thought it would.

'Let's have a look at it then,' said my mum. 'We should check that she's given you the right one.'

I put my hand into the paper bag and pulled the record from its sleeve. Two discs came out. The punk had somehow given me *two* copies of 'This Ole House'! My mum and I looked at each other and grinned. Without saying another word, we turned and quickly began to walk away. But a step or two later, something made me look back over my shoulder. The punk behind the record counter was staring straight at me! She knew! The punk *knew* that I was about to sneak away with an extra record and now she was going to tell the police!

For a second, my feet froze and my face burned hot with shame and panic. Then the punk grinned, stuck up her thumb and gave me another wink.

I put my spare copy of 'This Ole House' into a paper bag and gave it to Kate. Kate was in my new class in my new primary school in Felixstowe and she was one of my new friends. After I gave her the Shakin' Stevens single, she became my best friend. Pretty soon, she introduced me to Adam and the Ants and we both forgot all about Shakin' Stevens.

Adam Ant was a punk and, ever since that cheeky wink in Woolworths, I quite liked punks. Even the spiky-haired rebels who sat scowling on the steps of Ipswich Town Hall no longer frightened me quite as much. But there was more to Adam than most other punks. In his pop videos, he was also a pirate, a charming prince and a highwayman. What more could any fan want from their favourite pop star?

One day when we were in Kate's house, she suggested that we show our respect for Adam by dressing up just like him.

'We'll look cool,' she said. 'And we'll be starting an ant invasion of Felixstowe.'

I turned the idea over in my mind. *An ant invasion of Felixstowe with me and Kate as the leaders!* It was a great idea! I agreed to give it a go.

But changing from a nine-year-old girl into an ant isn't anywhere near as easy as it sounds. We studied Kate's posters of Adam and realised that we didn't have any of the clothes or make-up that we needed. We would have to use a little imagination instead.

In a lot of the pictures, Adam Ant was wearing grand military uniforms of red, gold and black. We couldn't copy this, so we didn't try. Opting for a more casual style, we stuck to our normal jeans and T-shirts and jazzed them up by tying posh silky scarves around our upper arms. These scarves were borrowed from Kate's mum – with or without her knowledge.

Next, we had to think about our make-up. Kate had none of her own but, again, we borrowed whatever we could from Kate's mum. Taking turns in front of the dressing-table mirror, we gave ourselves sharp red cheekbones and dusty, dark eye sockets. Instantly, we looked older and tougher. It felt good but it wasn't enough.

'I want a white stripe,' I said. 'No one will know I'm Adam Ant if I haven't got a white stripe across my face.'

Kate agreed and said that she wanted one too. We

looked inside her mum's make-up bag for a white lipstick but she didn't have one. In the end, we drew red stripes across our faces instead. It wasn't quite right but it was better than nothing.

Last of all, we looked at Adam's hair. He had black curls that were twisted into little plaits which fell on to his forehead. It was a really lovely detail and would be the perfect finish to our make-over. But after trying for ages to plait each other's short straight hair, Kate and I finally gave up. Then I had a brain wave. 'What we need are those little ties that you get on bread bags,' I said.

Quickly, we ran downstairs to the kitchen. There was a loaf of sliced bread still inside its polythene wrapper on the kitchen worktop. Twisted around one end of the wrapper and keeping the bread fresh was a little white strip of wire and plastic. Carefully, I undid it and twisted it into Kate's fringe instead. Kate now had a plait. Sort of.

After poking around in the bin, we found a plait for me too. Now we were ready to walk into town and begin our ant invasion.

Kate lived only a couple of streets away from Felixstowe town centre but, that day, the walk seemed to take longer than usual. Everyone we passed looked at us and laughed. When we reached the high street, it was no better. People were still pointing at us and laughing and one woman told us that we looked sweet. *Sweet?* She was wrong! We *didn't* look sweet. We looked dangerous and hard. We looked like punks. Even better than that, we looked like *ants*. But maybe Felixstowe wasn't ready for an ant invasion? Maybe Felixstowe wasn't ready for *us*? All I know for sure is that Kate and I never dressed up as ants again.

CHAPTER THREE

Me, My Mum and Barbra Streisand

At around the same time that I was falling in love with Shakin' Stevens and Adam Ant, I briefly became obsessed with Barbra Streisand. Barbra wasn't a rocker or a punk, she was a glamorous American actress who looked a bit like my Auntie Janice. But Barbra was also a singer and this was how she came to my attention. In 1980, her hit single 'Woman in Love' was number one in the UK charts for three weeks. It was a love song about a woman who would do *anything* to get her man into her world and keep him there. I ignored the song completely until I saw the video on *Top of the Pops*. Then I was spellbound.

Just picture the scene. Barbra is wearing an orange turban and riding a horse through a desert. It is a lonely landscape of sand, sky and mountains but Barbra isn't on her own. On another horse, a man rides with her. He has a big beard and wears a cape which is billowing out behind him. Suddenly, the desert and the mountains and the horses vanish, and Barbra and the hairy man are kissing on a bed. Then they are kissing in a soapy bathtub. Next, they kiss in the middle of a windstorm. Barbra's voice sings on and on over the top, getting higher and louder and more and more passionate. Then, all too soon, the music fades away and the kissing is over.

In 1980, that video was the most emotional thing I had ever seen.

For ages afterwards, I couldn't get Barbra's song out of my head. The powerful video had done its job and grabbed my interest, but it was the song itself which was the real hook. There was something addictive about the tune. It went round and round and up and up just like the spiral staircase on a helter-skelter. I started humming the tune at school and in my house, and soon I was humming it wherever I went. It wasn't going to take much to turn that hum into a roar.

One day, my mum took me shopping in a huge supermarket that she called the Cash and Carry. I hated going to ordinary supermarkets but I loved these rare trips to the Cash and Carry. Everything was sold in massive packs and this made shopping much more fun. If my mum wanted to buy a cake, she couldn't. She had to buy *ten* cakes instead. If she wanted to buy four cans of cola, she had to buy fifty.

To carry this much cake and cola, my mum pushed around a long wooden trolley which she let me stand on.

It was like being on a moving stage.

At some point during that shopping trip, I heard Barbra Streisand's song playing faintly in the background. Instead of humming, I started singing and, straightaway, I felt like I was in that video. Around me, the shelves of cake and cola and crisps and chocolate all melted away and were replaced by mountains and a hot sandy desert. The trolley became my horse. I threw open my arms and poured my heart and soul into that song.

On the other side of the trolley's handle, my mum started to giggle.

With one sneaky eye on my mum, I kept singing, higher and louder. I didn't know all the words so I filled in any gaps with heartfelt warbles or emotional shrieks. Soon, I was giving that song everything I had.

My mum's giggles got louder. 'Stop it, Hayley,' she said. 'Everyone is looking at us.'

I knew they were. That was the whole point! I was on a stage and I had an audience and I *was* Barbra Streisand. There was *no way* I was going to stop singing.

'Please,' begged my red-faced mum between giggles, '*please* shut up or I'm going to walk straight out of here and go back to the car.'

But with each *shut up*, I just got louder and more dramatic. I was a woman in love and I would NOT shut up.

My stunning performance lasted as far as the check-out and then I ran out of steam, exhausted by the drama of my performance. I can't remember if the check-out girl had been lucky enough to hear me sing but I will never forget my mum's laughter. For me, that will always be the real magic of that song.

CHAPTER FOUR
Fan Clubs

Before there was Twitter, Facebook or even that thing called The Internet, there were fan clubs. Joining a fan club was the only way you could learn more about your favourite pop stars and feel like you were part of a special gang. To join a fan club, you had to send a cheque to an address that you found in the back of *Smash Hits* and then wait a few weeks for your special fan club magazine – or *fanzine* – to arrive. It was a slow and sometimes costly business. When I was eleven, I took a short cut and started a fan club all by myself.

Actually, that's not quite true. I had help. That help came from Sarah.

Sarah and I met on the first day of high school. We were in the same tutor group and every morning we sat next to each other as the teacher took the register. I couldn't sit next to my old friend Kate because Kate had gone to another school and, for a while, I felt a bit lost without her. Nobody could ever be as cool as Kate. My life was ruined. Then, one morning, I noticed that Sarah had drawn a big letter M on her schoolbag. On top of the M was a funny little hat. This could only mean one thing. Madness.

Madness were my new favourite band. They weren't

rockers or punks or even ants – they were nutty boys. In their videos, the seven nutty boys of Madness wore Doc Marten boots, pork pie hats and drainpipe trousers. Being a nutty boy looked like fun, especially to a nutty girl like me.

I pointed at the graffiti on Sarah's bag and said, 'Did you do that?'

Sarah shrugged and nodded.

I nodded too, impressed. Then I asked a very silly question. 'Do you like Madness then?'

Sarah nodded again.

I smiled. I was a nutty girl and Sarah was a nutty girl and fate had put us in the same class at school! How fantastic and lucky was that!

Right there and then, the Orwell High School branch of The Madness Fan Club was born.

Our first fanzine was ten pages long and took us a whole weekend to make. We had no computer or typewriter, just a box of felt-tip pens. On the front cover, Sarah drew the same symbol that she'd drawn on her schoolbag and above that, in capital letters, she wrote THE MADNESS FAN CLUB: ISSUE #1. There could be no mistake about what was inside. Fans of Bucks Fizz and Cliff Richard should stay away.

Inside, we filled every page with our neatest handwriting. There were song lyrics that we copied from *Smash Hits* and some nutty facts that we either knew or just made up. There was also a giant word search and a quiz. The prize for the quiz was the seven-inch single of 'House of Fun'. It was Sarah's own record and she said that she didn't mind giving it away in order to help get our fan club off the ground. This was very generous of her. I don't think I would have given it away if it were mine.

When we'd filled the pages of one magazine, we gave it to Sarah's grandad who took it to work and photocopied ten more for us. Including our master copy, this meant that we now had eleven fanzines. So far, so good.

But then we started making mistakes.

'Do you think we should charge people a lump sum to join our club?' I asked. 'Or should we just sell our fanzines to anyone who wants one?'

We thought about it. It seemed easier just to take the fanzines to school and flog them at break-time. But how much should we sell them for?

'We can't ask too much,' I said. 'Nobody will want one if it means that they can't get a KitKat.' This was a very important point. The KitKat vending machine in our school sold rare three-finger KitKats for 20p each. That break-time KitKat was often the highlight of everyone's day.

Sarah scratched her head. 'Maybe we should include a free gift as well? Something to eat?'

This seemed like a great idea. We walked to the nearest shop and spent our pocket money on a big bag of Bazooka bubble gums, each one wrapped in its own blue and red wrapper. Then we taped a bubble gum to the front cover of each of our eleven fanzines. They looked great. If I wasn't selling them, I would definitely have been first in the queue to buy one.

But we still hadn't set a price.

After more head-scratching, we agreed on 10p.

The first issue of our fanzine sold out in seconds. We got rid of all eleven magazines, an entire bag of bubble gum and one seven-inch single of 'House of Fun'. In return, we made £1.10 to split between us. The Madness Fan Club was a runaway success.

Our classmates were hungry for more. One of them asked, 'When's the next issue coming out?'

'Next month,' I said.

There were a few groans and unhappy faces. 'That's ages away,' someone else said. 'We might not even like Madness by then.'

'OK, next week,' I said.

Sarah and I spent the whole of the following weekend working on Issue Number Two. We stuck to the same winning format. Our fanzine was filled with nutty facts, song lyrics, a word search and a prize quiz.

This time, it was my turn to provide the prize. I went to Woolworths, bought a high quality blank cassette and took it home to make a Madness mix tape. It wasn't as good as a seven-inch single but it wasn't bad!

'We should probably have a free gift again,' said Sarah. 'Maybe it should be something with a Madness logo on?'

I agreed. We returned to town and bought a big box of pencils and some plain white sticky labels. On each sticky label, we carefully drew a little M and a tiny pork pie hat. Then we curled a sticker around the top of each pencil and suddenly we had made our own Madness Fan Club pencils!

Sarah's grandad took our new issue to work and made us ten more copies. We took them to school and sold them instantly. In total, we had now got rid of ...

twenty-two magazines,
an entire bag of bubble gum,
one seven-inch single of 'House of Fun',
one *C60 TDK* cassette tape (top quality – no rubbish),

a box of brand new pencils,
a packet of sticky labels
and two entire weekends.

In return, we had made £2.20 to split between us.

The Madness Fan Club of Orwell High School was short-lived. The fanzine ran for only three or four issues before Sarah and I decided to quit. Our fanzines were a work of art and beauty but we were burnt out and broke. The saddest thing is that after all our hard work, we never kept a single copy of any one of those handmade magazines for ourselves. I would give almost anything to see one of them again. I would give a lot more than 10p, that's for sure!

After the rise and fall of the Madness Fan Club, I stayed away from the business side of things and started *joining* fan clubs instead. Convinced that I would one day marry George Michael, I began with Wham. After waiting several weeks, an envelope with my name on it plopped on to our doormat. Inside, there was a poster and a Christmas single. When I played the single, I heard a short thank you message. I was disappointed. I'd been hoping to hear a brand new song.

I went off Wham and became a member of the Howard Jones fan club. Howard Jones made cool electro-pop and had trendy hair. Also, he was Welsh and I liked that. Maybe he knew Shakin' Stevens? I found the address I needed, sent off my money and waited. Several weeks later, I received another envelope. This one contained a pretend VIP tour pass and another thank you message.

I went off Howard Jones and joined the Michael Jackson fan club. Michael Jackson was better than Wham *and* Howard Jones. He was the king of pop! Again, I sent off my money and waited. And I waited. And I waited. My envelope must have got lost in the post because nothing ever came back.

That was the last fan club I joined. But it didn't mean that I'd stopped loving music. Far from it. I was only just warming up.

CHAPTER FIVE
Radio

Between the ages of thirteen and sixteen, I spent a lot of time alone in my bedroom. If I wasn't at school or eating my tea that was almost certainly where I was. My early teenage years were not very exciting.

But this Bedroom Phase was actually a vital part of my development. Behind the closed door of my room, I was doing something very important. I was listening to the radio.

As the 1980s ticked on, I listened to the radio more and more. Until I was thirteen, I'd only ever known Radio 1. It woke me up in the morning, it was there when I came home from school and it was there at the weekend. I knew the voices of all the DJs and I knew exactly what songs to expect. Sometimes, I switched the radio on and sometimes I chose to put my record player on instead. Radio or record player – it didn't really make much of a difference. It was all Wham, Howard Jones and Michael Jackson anyway.

Then one day in 1984, a new radio station came on the air. It was called Laser 558 and I knew about it because one of my teachers mentioned it.

'You might be aware of a new radio station,' he said helpfully to my class. 'It's being broadcast from a ship just a few miles off the coast. They're pirates and they're breaking the law. It's illegal rubbish – don't listen to it.'

As soon as school was over, I rushed home and went straight up to my bedroom. Carefully, I turned the dial of my radio, sending the signal past a lot of random high-pitched squeals and hissing, until I got to 558. The first thing I heard was an American voice. This was new! I'd never heard an American DJ on my radio before.

'I'm Charlie Sea Wolf,' he said, 'and you're listening to Laser.'

Charlie *Sea* Wolf? This was new too. I thought DJs were almost always called Mike or Simon.

'You're never more than a minute away from music,' said Charlie Sea Wolf. 'So here are The Doors.'

The Doors? I'd never heard of them. I turned the volume up a little higher, sat closer to the radio and gave it my full attention. A crazy tune started playing on an electric organ. It was somehow weird and cheerful all at once, like a jingle you might hear blaring out of an ice-cream van. After a second or two, the crazy keyboard calmed down and was joined by a moody bass line. A man began to sing and my body broke out in goose bumps. He had the most beautiful and dangerous voice I had ever heard. I couldn't move. I could hardly even breathe! It felt like I was watching that video for 'Woman in Love' all over again.

The man sang a couple of verses and then he took a break and let the keyboard player take over. It sounded just like Dr. Teeth from *The Muppet Show* was playing the keyboards because they went on and *on* and got crazier and crazier. This was a *long* record! I looked at the clock. Entire minutes were passing and *still* the keyboard player kept playing. Where was the singer? Just as I was beginning to lose hope of ever hearing him again, he was suddenly back. He sang another verse or two, his voice rising to a howl before it faded into a groan. The ice-cream van returned with its mad jingle. And then ... with a grand drum roll, the record was over. I looked back at the clock and did some quick maths. This weird and wonderful song was at least seven minutes long.

'And that,' said Charlie Sea Wolf, 'was "Light My Fire".'

'Light My Fire' by The Doors. I carefully filed this information in my head for future use.

'This is Laser 558 and you're never more than a minute away from music,' said my new friend Charlie. 'And now here's Aretha Franklin with "Rock Steady". Don't go away.'

I didn't.

I stayed with Laser 558 right until it stopped broadcasting near the end of 1985. Looking back on it now, I can't believe that my favourite ever radio station was only on air for about eighteen months. But what an eighteen months it was! In that short time, Charlie and his fellow pirates broadened my mind and had a massive impact on my relationship with music. I heard hits from the 60s and Motown. I heard hip-hop and funky R&B. I heard Iggy Pop and The Pointer Sisters and Joy Division.

Even so, I didn't completely wave goodbye to Radio 1. Every Sunday at 5pm, I re-tuned my radio so that I could listen to the Top 40 countdown. When that was over, I left the radio dial exactly where it was for *The Annie Nightingale Request Show*. Annie was so cool that she started her show before she even said hello. The opening chords of a song would fill my bedroom and then, a split second before anyone started to sing, Annie interrupted with a lazy *Hi*. She timed it perfectly every single time.

One day, she began her show with a song called '7 Teen' by a band called The Regents. It was an instant hit with me. As I listened to the lyrics, I dreamt it was all about *me*, even though I *wasn't* seventeen. I wasn't even *six*teen. I was actually fourteen and I looked about twelve. So much for reality! Sometimes, it's easier to sit by the radio, close your eyes and dream.

For a while then, my best friends were Charlie Sea Wolf

and Annie Nightingale. This was a pretty tragic state of affairs! But my lonely teenage self should not have worried. All this time spent sitting in my room and listening to music was like paying money into the bank. One day, I'd get it all back with interest when I met people who had been listening to the same stuff as me.

And that day was just a Saturday job away.

CHAPTER SIX
Shop Music

'HAYLEY! PUT SOME MUSIC ON! PEOPLE WILL THINK THEY'VE WANDERED INTO A FLIPPING BOOK SHOP!'

It was Jeanie, my manageress. Her head was poking through the long strips of plastic that hung from the doorway of the stockroom and she was waving her finger at the silent stereo on the ledge behind me. Before I could open my mouth and make any sort of reply, Jeanie pulled her neck back through the plastic curtain and vanished.

I quickly finished lacing up a trainer, thrust it into the hands of my waiting customer and rushed across the shop and into the stockroom. Then I ran through the twisting maze of shoeboxes to Jeanie's office and knocked on the door.

'COME IN.'

I pushed the door open. Jeanie was sitting at her desk. She looked at me, rolled her eyes and said, 'Hayles, what have I told you about leaving the shop unattended?'

'Sorry,' I said, and then got straight to the point. 'Can I choose?'

Jeanie looked confused. 'Eh? Choose what?'

'The music?' I crossed my fingers. 'Can *I* choose it

this time?'

Jeanie was silent for a moment and then she gave a snort of laughter. 'Of course you can, love. You can choose anything you like as long as it's Elton John.'

I was sixteen and I'd been working as a Saturday girl in a shoe shop for a couple of months. If Saturday jobs could be rated, this one would get three stars. It had three major plus points in its favour and each one was worth a star.
1. I didn't have to wear a uniform.
2. I got paid £1.64 an hour.
3. I liked looking at all the different boots and shoes.

On the down side, there was Jeanie and Elton John. Jeanie's love for Elton John was unhealthy. She wouldn't let us listen to anyone else. After only a few Saturdays, this situation was driving me nuts.

Then one day, something happened which eased the tension and earned my job another star. Another Saturday girl came to join us.

This new girl was called Noz and she was in the year below me at school. Very quickly, I learned that my greater age was not an advantage. While I was still shuffling around in a pair of scuffed slip-ons and a pencil skirt, Noz had already waved goodbye to high-street fashion and found a style of her very own. Her hair was dyed a different colour every week and she wore heavy eyeliner and clothes that came from charity shops. Best of all were the bovver boots on her feet. Noz walked like a winner and there was no way that she was ever going to shuffle around on pin heels.

'They're monkey boots,' she told me, when I asked. 'You get them from the Army and Navy Shop.'

Noz knew all about The Doors. She even knew about The Regents! Noz was a hippy rock chick and her knowledge of pop music marked her out as a child of Charlie Sea Wolf and Annie Nightingale. Just like me! Elton was still lurking in the background, but my Saturdays became brilliant.

Then one Saturday we arrived at work to find that Jeanie wasn't there. She'd left the shoe shop forever and she'd taken all her Elton John cassettes with her. In her place was a new manageress called Dee. Dee was hardly any older than me and loved Lionel Richie, Luther Vandross and nightclubbing. What she definitely *didn't* love was Saturday mornings. Every Saturday began with the same conversation:

Dee: If you need me, I'll be in the office doing the accounts. [Big yawn] But make sure you bang loudly on the door – don't just walk in.

Us: We won't.

Dee: Are you sure you'll be OK out here on your own?

Us: We will.

Dee: OK, don't mess around and don't forget to put some music on. But stick to *my* tapes, please. No sneaking on any weird stuff.

Us: We won't.

Dee: [Another big yawn] Cheers, girls. I'll see you later.

With that, Dee would stumble off to her office. We rarely saw her again before 2pm. Noz and I ruled the shoe shop and my Saturday job was now worthy of the full five stars.

At first, we did exactly as we were told and played only Dee's cassettes. As well as Lionel Richie and Luther Vandross, Dee had *all* eleven volumes of *Now That's What I Call Music!* Each of these double cassettes had thirty chart hits on them. That added up to a *lot* of music. But it wasn't enough music for us.

After a couple of Saturdays, we started playing tapes of our own. The shoe shop now rocked to the sound of The Doors and David Bowie and Heart and Janis Joplin. I ditched my pencil skirt and scruffy slip-ons and got myself a charity shop dress and a pair of monkey boots instead. The volume of the stereo crept up and whenever we weren't selling shoes, we were dancing.

One Saturday, I came back from my lunchbreak with a tape that I'd bought in Woolworths. It was *Hatful of Hollow* by The Smiths. Everyone knew about The Smiths. They were the weirdest band in Britain but also the coolest. Morrissey, the singer, had a huge quiff and wore a hearing aid even though he didn't need one. In every song, he sounded depressed. I loved him.

'We probably shouldn't play that in here,' said Noz, who was hurrying past the till with a shoe in her hand. 'I don't think Dee would like it.'

I looked at the clock. It wasn't time for Dee to wake up yet and there was only one customer in the shop anyway. *One song couldn't hurt, could it?* I took the tape out of its case and shoved it into the cassette player.

There was a moment of silence as the fresh tape whirled around the cassette heads and then I heard the opening chords of 'Heaven Knows I'm Miserable Now'. I frowned. This wasn't the song I'd been expecting. For some reason, we'd skipped straight to side 2. I shrugged and let the tape play on. The shop filled with the sound of a jangly guitar and, soon afterwards, Morrissey began to wail and moan in his own unique way. I crossed my arms on the shop's counter, rested my chin on my wrist and listened.

When I next looked up, Noz was hugging a box of unsold shoes and trying very hard not to laugh. Meanwhile, our only customer was stuffing his feet back into his trainers. 'I CAN'T STAY IN HERE WITH THIS CRAP MUSIC ON,' he said angrily. Then he marched straight out of the shop and was gone.

Noz and I looked at each other and started to laugh. What a result!

The Smiths 1 – Customers 0

After that, it became a game. There were three simple rules.

1. Give everyone in the shop a lovely surprise.

2. Make each other laugh.

3. Get rid of as many customers as possible.

At first, we stuck to The Smiths. Loud blasts of 'HEAVEN KNOWS I'M MISERABLE NOW' filled the shop whenever it got too busy. Imagine Yazz singing, 'The only way is up'... and 'HEAVEN KNOWS I'M MISERABLE NOW'. That kind of thing.

Soon, we branched out and added whatever weirdness we could find. A particular favourite was a massive slice of Europop by a German band called Opus. Rather oddly, the song was called 'Live is Life' and it had a clap-along rhythm and a big chorus of 'La... laaa... la la la'. Every so often, one of us would sneak over to the stereo and put it on while the other person was busy with a customer. When that marvellous song exploded through the speakers, it never failed to make us both shake with laughter. It was childish but it was funny.

All good things must come to an end. After a year or so, I waved goodbye to my Saturday job so that I could go to university. But even though I left the shoe shop forever, it never fully left me. If I close my eyes, I can take myself back there in an instant. I'm sixteen years old, and me and Noz are pocketing £1.64 an hour and dancing to The Doors and laughing.

It was the worst paid job I'd ever have but it was also one of the best.

CHAPTER SEVEN
Hits and Mixtapes

When I was in the second year of sixth form, my form tutor gave me some handy advice on how to choose the right university. 'Don't get bogged down by frills and extra details,' he said. 'Wherever you go, you're going there to get a degree so the only thing that *really* matters is the course. It's *all* about the course.'

'Thank you,' I said, nodding. 'I'll make sure I do some proper research.'

My tutor was a nice man. He gave me a handbook which named all the universities in order from A to Z and listed the courses that they offered. All I had to do next was compare every single English Literature course in Britain and choose the one that I liked the most. 'It might take a while,' my tutor told me. 'But it'll be worth it in the end.'

I took the handbook away and began at the beginning. A was for ...

Aberdeen University.

Aberdeen? That was up in Scotland, wasn't it? However great the English course was, it seemed like a very long way to go. Also, it would be freezing cold and it would probably snow a lot. I turned to the next page.

Aberystwyth, University College of Wales.

Aber-*where?* A quick look in my dad's road atlas showed me that it was nearly three hundred miles away and in Wales. To everyone's surprise and mine as well, I chose that one. To this day, I'm not sure why.

Maybe it was because I'd had lovely holidays in Wales as a child?

Or maybe I was still a little bit in love with Shakin' Stevens?

Or perhaps I was just too plain lazy to look at another page of that boring handbook?

Whatever the reason, I'm sure it had very little to do with the English Literature course. It didn't matter. It was the right move anyway, even if it was a hasty and rather random decision. Then again, maybe some strange forces were at work and it was always meant to be that way. Maybe Aberystwyth was written in my stars.

Leaving home was exciting but there were a couple of things that I found difficult. One of them was choosing which tapes to take with me. I only had enough space to take a few so I began with *the best*.

The Best of Blondie by Blondie

The Very Best of The Doors by The Doors

The Beatles 1967–1970 by The Beatles

The World Won't Listen by The Smiths

They were all greatest hits collections, even the one by The Smiths. Hits albums weren't very cool but I packed them anyway. It seemed like the best use of my limited space.

It wasn't.

A diet of constant hits quickly started to make me feel sick. The balance was wrong. It was like eating jam every day without a doughnut or drinking too much vodka without any tonic.

Luckily, I'd also packed a handful of mixtapes. These were filled with the B-sides of singles and favourite album tracks and even songs I'd taped from the radio. Making a mixtape took time and skill. You had to make sure that the end of one song worked well with the start of another. It was all about getting things in exactly the right order.

The best mixtapes were always the ones that had been made for me by someone else. These were unique delights.

Shoe Shop Classics from Noz.

University Will Tear Us Apart from my sixth-form boyfriend.

I didn't just love listening to these tapes, I loved *looking* at them too. The inlay cards were covered in scribbly handwriting and often decorated with doodles. In a world without mobile phones or FaceTime, these mixtapes passed on a very special message. They said, 'I have spent at least an hour of my life making this tape for you because you are worth it.'

Make no mistake, a mixtape was a very beautiful gift. And if it came in the post with a letter, it was even better.

The other tricky thing about leaving home was getting through Freshers' Week. My first seven days at university were a blur of new faces and a constant string of questions.

What's your name?

What subject are you doing?

What A Levels did you get?

Where are you from?

So what music do you like?

Are you really 18? You look about 12.

I answered all the questions and tagged on to anyone who talked to me, but inside I was secretly screaming. *These are not my kind of people*, I thought. *Can I truly be friends with anyone who blasts Elton John from their room?* Without my mixtapes and my memories, I might have given up and gone straight home.

Luckily, my panic was short-lived and ended almost as soon as it began. Before the week was over, I had a whole new set of fabulous friends. I didn't find them in my accommodation block or in the English Department or at any of the Freshers' Fairs ...

I found them where the music was.

CHAPTER EIGHT
Jukebox

The Central Hotel in Aber was more like a pub than a hotel. It smelt of stale beer and spilled cider and the whole place was heaving with drunk students. I pushed myself into a gap in front of the bar and stood on tiptoes hoping to get served.

It was still Freshers' Week. Or at least, I *think* it was. I was feeling so swamped by the newness of it all that I'd lost track of time. I'd been on walking tours and coach trips. I'd stood in slow-moving queues and signed endless forms. I'd been to welcome lectures and Freshers' Fairs. I'd joined three clubs.

The West Wales Wanderers (a walking group)

The Aber Caving Club (I don't like the dark)

The Rock Society (music – not big stones)

And now I was on a pub crawl with a crowd of people whose names I'd soon forget. I fixed a smile on my face and hoped that the barman would hurry up and serve me. I *needed* a pint of liquid in my hands. It would make it harder for me to rush out the door and run away.

To my relief, the barman spotted me and a minute or two later I was pushing my way back through the crowds and clutching a pint of cider and blackcurrant.

My fellow pub-crawlers were huddled in a corner, deep in conversation.

'We were just saying,' one of them said, putting her mouth to my ear, 'how much we're all missing our boyfriends.'

'Oh.' I took a sip of my cider.

'Have *you* got a boyfriend back home?'

I took another sip. 'Yeah ... well, no ... well ... off and on ... ' My voice trailed away. We'd had this conversation before.

The Girl with the Boyfriend said something to her mates and they all looked at me and nodded. 'In a way, I *envy* you,' said yet another Girl with a Boyfriend. 'Don't get me wrong, I *love* Lance ... but being away from home is so much *harder* when you're in a serious relationship.'

I didn't know what to say to this but luckily it didn't matter. My companions were now giving each other a group hug. I looked wistfully around the bar of the Central Hotel and wondered why EVERY SINGLE PERSON was having a better time than me.

Suddenly, I put my glass down on a table. 'I'll be back in a bit,' I said to the huggers. 'I need the loo.'

Actually, I just needed to escape. This was no good at all. In fact, it was close to terrible. Forgetting all about my promise to return, I put my head down and made a beeline for the Central's front door. But then I stopped.

Over the laughter and chatter and shouts of the students, a record had started to play. It was 'Heaven Knows I'm Miserable Now'.

Never had a song sounded so right.

I smiled and lifted my head. And that was when I saw it! Somehow, in spite of all the bodies blocking my way, I caught a glimpse of a jukebox. It wasn't even a big upright modern one with flashing lights. It was just a glass box about half as big as me and it was all lit up and pulling me towards it like a magnet.

My feet instantly changed direction.

When I got to the jukebox, there was a group of girls and lads hanging around next to it. They were using it as a table to rest their pint glasses on.

'Excuse me,' I said. 'Do you mind if I put a record on?'

One of the boys said something in Welsh and laughed but he picked up his glass and moved aside anyway. One of the girls said, 'Go for it. Most of them are older than my dad, though.'

I smiled and shrugged and looked down at my options. The girl was right. The records *were* old and what's more, they were *actually* records. There were no CDs here. This glass-sided jukebox was filled with a stack of 7-inch vinyl singles. The names of each single and its B-side were written in biro on rows of glowing buttons. All you had to do was press the button of the song that you wanted.

| ROD STEWART | A: *The Killing of Georgie part 1* |
| | B: *The Killing of Georgie part 2* |

| DIRE STRAITS | A: *Money for Nothing* |
| | B: *Love Over Gold* (*live*) |

| GEORGE MICHAEL | A: *Careless Whisper* |
| | B: *Instrumental* |

I read every single label – even the B-sides. I took such a long time that The Smiths finished playing before I pushed a button. But finally I did and it was this one:

| THE ZOMBIES | A: *She's Not There.* |

It was a Laser 558 favourite and it was two and a half minutes of perfect pop from the 1960s. Inside the jukebox, my chosen single was raised up by a robotic arm and then flipped over on to a spinning turntable. I watched, unable to pull my eyes away.

The record started to play and the Central Hotel was filled with the sweet sound of The Zombies.

'Oh, *lush* choice!' I looked up. It was the girl who had spoken before. She was grinning from ear to ear and nodding her head to the Zombie beat. 'I *love* this track,' she said. '*Stonking!*'

I smiled. This girl had the best accent I'd ever heard in my life and she had new words too. *Stonking?*

The Welsh-speaking boy now said something in English. 'Who is this band again? Is it The Turtles?'

'No, it's The Zombies,' I said.

'That's right,' he said, and slapped his palm against the side of his head. 'I knew that.'

'Like hell you did, Rhys,' said another one of the girls.

'Shut up, Lynda,' said Rhys, and pulled a face.

Lynda stuck her middle finger up at Rhys and then stretched out her arms and started dancing. She twirled round and round with a pint glass in her hand, forcing everyone else out of the way until she had her very own dance floor in front of the jukebox. When the music stopped, someone shoved a coin in the jukebox and put the same record on again.

Lynda just kept on twirling!

Before The Zombies could finish their song a second time, me and Rhys and the rest of this cheerful gang were twirling around and dancing with her.

At last, I'd found my kind of people.

CHAPTER NINE
The Blues

There is some music that I can't listen to any more.

In my second term at university, my parents' marriage ended. I fed fifty pences into pay phones while queuing students tapped on the glass and told me to hurry up. But I couldn't hurry up because some conversations can't be rushed. All I could do was listen from a distance as my family fell apart. I was almost three hundred miles away. I felt glad and guilty about that, in equal measure.

To numb the guilt, I went out more and drank more cider than was good for me. I got up late, missed lectures and lived on Pot Noodles and chocolate. My weight dipped to six and a half stone.

At some point during that second term, a kind guy who taught me American Literature asked me if I was OK. I said no and started to cry.

The university arranged a transfer for me. All I had to do was finish my first year and then I could move to Essex University instead, where I'd be closer to home. I kept on shoving coins into pay phones and drank even more cider.

One warm day in late spring, my friend Lynda knocked on my door holding a big tub of ice-cream. A little surprised, I let her in. I didn't often see Lynda on her own.

We always hung out in a big group.

We sat on my bed and ate the ice-cream straight from the tub with two spoons. I was just starting to feel sick when Lynda said, 'Do you really want to leave Aber?'

'No,' I said.

Lynda shrugged and lobbed a spoonful of ice-cream straight out of my open window. We heard somebody swear outside. 'Then don't,' she said. It was the best piece of advice anyone has ever given me.

After that, I followed Lynda around like a shadow. She didn't seem to mind. She was studying Fine Art and she let me watch TV in her room while she painted. Sometimes, we listened to music instead. Lynda liked weird arty bands I'd never heard of. There was one band she played more than any other. They were called This Mortal Coil and their music was as strange as their name.

'*This Mortal Coil?*' I said. 'What does that even *mean*?'

Lynda chewed the end of her paintbrush and looked thoughtful. 'It means we're all going to die,' she said, and then she laughed.

I frowned and listened to the song on the tape. Strictly speaking, it wasn't even a song because there weren't any words. It was just a piece of music – the sort that could empty a shoe shop in seconds. Scratching my head, I said, 'What exactly is it that you like about this?'

Lynda stopped painting and looked thoughtful again.

She pointed at her stereo with her paintbrush and said, 'It's coming up right now – listen.'

I listened. Two droning notes filled the room.

Lynda nodded and smiled. '*That* bit reminds me so much of the foghorn I used to hear on foggy mornings when I stayed at my nana's house in South Shields. When I play this tape, it takes me straight back there – like time travel.'

I stared at her, speechless.

Lynda bit her lip and then let out a giggle. 'You think I'm nuts now, don't you?'

I shook my head. 'No,' I said, a smile growing on my face. 'I think we're the same.'

Many years have passed since then and Lynda and I are still great friends. Although we live a long way apart, we talk to each other almost every week. Lynda still paints and she still listens to This Mortal Coil. I can't ever listen to them again. They remind me too much of that time when I almost dropped out.

CHAPTER TEN
Rock Nights

In the early 1990s, Aber didn't have a single nightclub. That was fine by me. I didn't like them anyway. Who cared about dolling yourself up to go to Chicagos or Hollywoods or Miami Nights when you could dance in your jeans down at the Footy Club? In fact, we were spoilt for choice. Let me introduce ...

Hayley's Guide to Going Out in Aber at the Start of the 90s

The Footy Club
The clubhouse of the mighty Aberystwyth Town FC. Saturday nights only. Over by midnight. Lots of Roxette and Madonna.

Downstairs at the Bay Hotel
A disco in a basement. If it wasn't horribly crowded, it was completely dead. The DJ had the 12-inch mix of 'Tainted Love' by Soft Cell.

Skinners
As grim as it sounded. Basically, the bar and disco were outside in a courtyard. Often very cold.

Rock Night at the Angel Hotel
Every Wednesday in the back room of a pub. Lots of hairy men. Lots of Iron Maiden and Motorhead.

Rummers

Dancing on a sawdust-covered floor to a lone bloke with a guitar. Usually that bloke was called Phil Fernando. Good old Phil!

The Up Top Bop

Saturday night in the Student Union. *The* place to be. Tickets went on sale Wednesday and were sold out by Thursday. Lazy grooving to The Stone Roses and the Happy Mondays. Bring it on!

Rock Night in the Student Union

Live music every Friday. Usually a rock band but not always. Usually enjoyable but not always.

House Parties

Often ended early after a polite visit from the police.

House parties in Aber were crazy, cramped and airless. They reminded me of a game I sometimes played in primary school. It was called the Matchbox Game. The teacher gave everyone an empty matchbox and the winner was whoever could cram it full with the highest number of random tiny objects. Aber house parties were just like this but bigger. Instead of a matchbox we had a house and instead of random tiny objects we had human beings. Whenever I went to a party, I never stayed long. I just can't enjoy myself if I can't breathe.

For me, it was all about Fridays. In our second year, Lynda and I spent our student loans on tickets to gigs. We never saw anyone famous and that was half the fun. The bands who came to Aber had names we'd never heard of and that we quickly forgot again. Walking through the doors of the Student Union on a Friday night was like walking into the unknown. Anything could happen.

One day, we went to see a band called Lawnmower Deth. *Deth* not death. Don't ask me what *Deth* means because I don't know. Also, don't ask me why we bought tickets to go and see them because I can't answer that either. But we did and I'm glad of it. It turned out to be one of the greatest nights of my life.

There weren't many girls in the union that night. The fans of Lawnmower Deth were mostly very pale boys who looked like they needed a hot bath and a meal. Lynda and I got our drinks from the bar, stood in a gap at the front of the stage and waited as the hall filled up. At last, the lights dimmed and the band appeared. They were all lads and there were quite a few of them. One of them was wearing a pink tutu.

'I THINK THIS MIGHT BE GOOD,' said Lynda, shouting above the sound of the crowd.

The first song was called 'Weebles Wobble But They

Don't Fall Down'. It started like a bomb going off and it was so loud that I went dizzy with shock. But then Lynda nudged me and jerked her head at the crowd behind us. I looked around. The pale-faced boys had all dropped on to the floor and were lying on their backs with their legs in the air. Apart from us, the entire audience was a sea of kicking legs.

Lynda and I looked at each other over our plastic pint glasses and burst into laughter. The band kept playing and the singer kept shouting and the legs kept kicking. I was laughing so hard that my ribs hurt. Luckily, the song only lasted about half a minute. Then all the boys got back on to their feet and I was able to breathe again.

The singer burped into his microphone and said, 'This next one is a cover of the Led Zeppelin classic "Stairway to Heaven".'

I knew this song. It was another Annie Nightingale favourite. It was about eight or nine minutes long and began very slowly with a folk guitar and a flute.

'I THINK THIS MIGHT BE GOOD,' I shouted into Lynda's ear.

The band began to play. If we'd been standing next to a jet engine, it couldn't have been any noisier. I could feel the beat thumping through my body. All the boys started jumping up and down and bouncing into each other. Twenty seconds later, the song finished.

'And that,' said the singer, 'was a lot more fun than listening to Led Zeppelin for half your life. We don't want you to be bored tonight.'

The crowd roared in agreement. Me and Lynda started to laugh again.

'Don't forget that you can buy our album,' said the singer. 'It's called *Ooh Crikey!*'

For some reason, this made me and Lynda laugh even harder. I think I was crying.

The singer said, 'This next one is called "Fish Dance". So down you go again, folks.'

The deafening racket returned and around us, everyone dropped down on to their backs and kicked their legs up into the air. This time, me and Lynda shoved our glasses on to the stage and joined in. Dancing like fish felt like the right thing to do. Besides, we were laughing so hard that we could hardly stand up anyway.

We're still laughing about that night even now.

CHAPTER ELEVEN

Our Tune

Everyone has a song that reminds them of love or heartbreak. I have an entire album.

In my third year at university, I fell in love. I'd dabbled with romance before but I wasn't any good at it. After a few dates and phone calls, I'd start feeling twitchy and trapped and then I'd end it.

This was different.

He worked in a chip shop in Aber and I met him in the downstairs disco of the Bay Hotel. As far as I was concerned, it was love at first sight. He had dark blond hair that fell down to his jawline and he looked like a rock star.

'Oh my gosh,' I said to Lynda. 'That guy over there is totally lush.'

'I dare you to go and talk to him,' she said.

On a normal night, I would have laughed at this madcap dare and ignored it. But this wasn't a normal night. All afternoon, we'd been at a beer festival. My brain and mouth weren't working in their usual way.

'OK,' I said. 'I will.' And that's what I did.

He was The One. I was sure of it. Even though he smelled strongly of chips, I got butterflies in my tummy whenever I saw him. He was older than me and he had a degree in history and could talk about books and art and important things that were going on in the world. He had piles and piles of LP records in his room. We lay on his bed and listened to post-punk bands like Television and Sonic Youth. We listened to American college rock like The Pixies and Throwing Muses. We listened to a young woman from the West Country called PJ Harvey. I *loved* PJ Harvey. I loved the chip shop guy too.

But after a month or so, I started feeling twitchy and trapped. And even though I saw them every day, I was missing my friends.

I tried to push these feelings out of my head. The chip shop guy was gorgeous. Why ruin a good thing?

One day, he knocked on the door of my room. When I saw him, my tummy filled up with butterflies again. This guy was a keeper! I needed to hang on to him and not mess this up.

'Hi,' he said. 'Have you got a few minutes?'

'Of course.' I waved him in and went to fill up my kettle.

Instead of sitting down, he stood awkwardly in the middle of my room. Then he dropped the bomb. 'Um ... the thing is ... I think we should stop seeing each other.'

I froze, kettle in hand. After a second of shocked silence, I said, '*Why?*'

The chip shop guy turned red and looked at his boots. 'I just don't think this is working. I don't think ... you're ... all that fussed about us.'

'I *am*,' I said. Then I bit my lip and felt shifty.

He shook his head. 'No you're not,' he said. 'You'd rather be out with your mates.' He shrugged and then smiled and pulled a small package out of his pocket. 'I've bought you something. I want you to have it so please take it.'

I put down my kettle and took the package from him. Although it was neatly wrapped up, I could tell right away that it was a cassette tape.

'Thanks,' I muttered.

The chip shop guy scratched his head and gave me a sorry half-smile. 'I'll be off,' he said. And then he kissed me quickly on the cheek and walked out of my life forever.

For a while I stood there with his wrapped gift in my hand. Then I opened it. I was right. It was a cassette tape, of course – and a really good one! It was the new album by a hot American band called Nirvana. I'd once told the chip shop guy that he looked a bit like Nirvana's singer, Kurt Cobain.

On the front of the tape's inlay card was an image of a swimming baby. I stared down at it and started to cry. But a few seconds later, I was laughing through my tears. I couldn't stop myself! The chip shop guy had dumped me with such style that I felt like clapping. His parting gift was perfect. He'd given me an album called *Nevermind*.

Never mind, eh?

CHAPTER TWELVE

Tanya

My life as a student ended just like a Nirvana track. There was no slow gentle fade-out. It was noisy, then it went quiet, then it went a bit wild and then it just stopped. One day I was living in Aber with my friends, and the next, it was time to pack up and go home.

With no clue about what to do next, I went back to my mum's and weighed up my options:

I could stay in Felixstowe and work in an office on the dock.

I could go back to Aber and work in a chip shop.

I could go somewhere else.

I chose option C. But first, I had to pay off my overdraft.

I got a job in a café. For several months I worked six days a week from seven until five. Most of that time I was doing the washing-up in a tiny kitchen that had no windows. To add to my fun, the owner of the café had a weird habit of placing a hand on my arm every time he walked past the sink. Let's call him Mr Tickle. That wasn't his only weird habit. He also played Shania Twain *all* the time. One day,

I spoke to him about this.

'She's *cheerful*,' he said, instantly turning pink and cross. 'Not like your depressing Nirvana or R.E.M. rubbish!'

'Yes, but ... but *all the time*?'

Mr Tickle gave a sulky shrug. 'I've got a few Elton John CDs too. Do you want me to put one of them on?'

For a moment I stared at the deep fat fryer and wondered whether I should throw myself into it. Then I said, 'It's OK – Shania is fine.'

Mr Tickle reached out and cupped my elbow. 'Good,' he said, smiling again, 'I think so too.' With that, he turned around, wiggled his big bottom at me and then danced out of the kitchen singing, 'Man! I Feel Like a Woman'.

It was a low point.

Luckily, there was a place just across the street which helped me to get through these dark days. It was the public library.

Every day after work I went and sat in there for a while. I had nothing else to do. All my school friends had left town and my old shoe shop buddy Noz was backpacking on the other side of the world. The library was a little island of hope. Also, you could borrow LP records for 50p.

One day I found something very special in there. In amongst all the scruffy old albums, there was one record that still looked brand new and untouched. I plucked it out of the rack and gave it a closer look. The LP cover was filled with an image of ghostly toy ballerinas and above them, the band's logo was floating like an airship.

'Belly,' I whispered, and then I squinted to read the album title which was printed in tiny letters just next to it. *Star*.

Flipping the record over in my hands, I looked at the tracks listed on the back. The first song was called 'Someone to Die For'. I smiled. It sounded like exactly the sort of song that Lynda would like. I dug 50p out of my purse and took the record to the desk.

It was love at first listen. That night I sat in my bedroom and listened to both sides of the LP and when I'd finished, I listened to it all over again. Then I went downstairs to the kitchen to phone my friend Lynda. 'I've been listening to this new album,' I said. 'It's called *Star* by Belly. Have you heard of it?'

'Yes,' said Lynda, far away in her parents' house in south Wales. 'It's Tanya Donelly's new band, isn't it? They're on the same record label as This Mortal Coil.'

I frowned. Lynda *always* knew more about music than me. Maybe it was because she was older and she'd been to art school? 'Oh,' I said. 'Well, anyway, this album is incredible.'

'What's it like?'

What was it like? I closed my eyes for a moment and rested the receiver against my cheek. How could I ever explain this weird, fun, strange, cheerful sound that I'd just heard? Lifting the phone to my ear again, I said, 'It's guitar pop but it's much *more* than that.' I took a deep breath and called on the ghosts of my English degree. 'It's like … it's like a woman wailing for her demon lover … but … but *tunefully*.'

On the other end of the phone, there was silence.

I bit my lip. 'I sound nuts, don't I?'

The phone line crackled and there was a chuckle in my ear. 'No,' said Lynda. 'You sound like me.'

I nodded, smiling. 'Hey Lynda, what did you say the singer's name was?'

'Tanya,' said my older, wiser friend. 'Tanya Donelly. Read your sleeve notes.'

I didn't just read the sleeve notes. If Belly were listed on a magazine cover, I bought it. If they had a single out, I bought that too. My borrowed album went back to the library after only seven days but my connection with Belly and Tanya Donelly was mine forever.

I bought my own copy of *Star* on vinyl and listened to

it so much that I still know every single word and every chord change. A few years later, I was given Belly's next album *King* on CD by a nice guy called Dave. I hadn't been going out with Dave and he wasn't dumping me – it was just a really great gift!

I bought CD singles and rare Japanese imports. When Belly broke up, I bought Tanya's solo albums. In between listening to these, I went backwards in time and bought albums by the bands she'd been in before she formed Belly.

I felt like Tanya was my friend. She *looked* like she should be my friend. In every picture I saw of her, she looked like just the sort of person who would have danced in the shoe shop with me and Noz or kicked her legs up in the air at a Lawnmower Deth gig.

The more I read about her, the better we got on. I learned that Tanya is from Boston and her nickname is Tee. I know that she's almost exactly five years older than me because we have almost the same birthday. I know she's married to Dean and she's got one, or maybe two, children. I know she's one of the coolest women in the world.

In 2016 Belly got back together again and went on tour. I went to see them in Norwich and stood right next to the stage with my friend Morgan. Tanya was just a couple of metres away, playing her guitar and singing and smiling and sometimes wailing. She looked the same as she did in 1993 – only this time, she was right in front of me.

In between songs, Gail Greenwood, the bass player, talked to the crowd. At one point, she said, 'It was Tanya's birthday a few days ago. She was fifty!'

Everyone cheered. Tanya shrugged like it was no big deal.

I cheered too but my cheers were mixed with amazement. I wanted to shout, 'IT'S MAD, ISN'T IT, TEE? HERE WE ARE, BOTH MIDDLE-AGED, AND IT WAS ONLY THE OTHER DAY THAT I FOUND YOU IN FELIXSTOWE LIBRARY!'

I didn't shout this of course. It would have made me sound nuts. I'm not nuts and I'm not a stalker. I just happen to have a very good friend who doesn't know I exist. I think that's pretty normal, isn't it?

CHAPTER THIRTEEN
Music On The Move

As soon as I'd paid off my overdraft, I packed up my Walkman and a handful of tapes and went somewhere else. In fact, I went to a lot of places. For the next four years, I moved from job to job and from country to country. I wasn't a rock star but I could still be a rolling stone!

First I went to a campsite in Brittany in the north-west of France. When I arrived on a chilly spring day, the campsite was little more than a few lonely fields. There were no tents, no camper-vans and no campers. The shower blocks were locked, the pool had no water in it and the bar and the shop were shut. My first task was to put up all the tents.

At least I wasn't doing this on my own. There was a whole team of us. We had travelled to France on the ferry from Southampton and were now zig-zagging around Brittany, moving from campsite to campsite and filling them with neat rows of tents. On each site, two or three members of our team were left behind so that our group was getting smaller and smaller and the work was getting harder and harder. Luckily for me, I was dropped off right near the top of the list. I didn't have to do this back-breaking work for very long.

But as more and more tents went up and the time for everyone to leave crept closer, I started to panic. I was being left in the middle of nowhere all on my own. The girl I was supposed to be working with hadn't arrived yet. What if she *never* arrived? Even worse, what if she *did* arrive and she was a serial killer?

Unable to contain my alarm, I came up with a new plan and spoke to Christine who was the head of our team. 'Can I stay here with John or Andi or Dan?' I asked. 'I *know* them. I don't know this other person. Why can't she go and work with someone else?'

Christine listened carefully and nodded. Then she said, 'Fiona is getting here tomorrow and she's working with *you*. So deal with it.'

I shut my mouth and went back to building my tents.

When Fiona arrived, she had a big smile on her face and a huge skull and crossbones on her sweatshirt. My gut instinct told me that she was far too cool to be a serial killer. I stopped sulking and gave her a tour of the campsite. I showed her the tents that would soon be filled with holidaymakers. I showed her the shower block and the closed bar and the shop that wasn't yet a shop. Then I showed her the scruffiest tent on the entire campsite. 'Um ... and this is where we live,' I said. 'Welcome to your new home.'

I followed Fiona through the zip-up doorway and

continued my guided tour inside. 'That's where we cook,' I said, and pointed to a camping stove on a set of wobbly metal shelves. Next, I pointed to another zip-up doorway. 'That's where we sleep,' I said, and gave her a sorry shrug.

Fiona shrugged back.

Finally, I waved my arm at a plastic table and chairs, adding, 'And this is ... well, this is the rest of it.'

There was nothing else to show her. No television. No radio. No anything. It was 1993 but we were almost living in the Stone Age.

Fiona looked around the tent and frowned. 'We need to go to Leclerc.'

'*Leclerc?*' It was my turn to frown.

'It's a big French supermarket,' she said. 'There's something we've got to buy *urgently*.'

I thought about my almost empty bank account and gave her a worried sideways glance. 'Is there?'

'Too right there is,' said Fiona, firmly. 'We need a stereo. I can't live without music.'

And BOOM! Right there, in that second, a beautiful friendship was formed.

We clubbed together and bought the cheapest stereo in the supermarket. It had two cassette decks and a radio.

The speakers were so bad that they buzzed and crackled whenever we turned the volume up. We didn't mind. We turned the volume up anyway and we pushed that cheap little machine to the limit.

For the next six months, our days were a loop of cleaning tents and chatting to holidaymakers and playing huge games of Hide and Seek in the woods. It was a dirty job but somebody had to do it!

In the evenings, Fiona and I ate sandwiches filled with chocolate ice-cream and drank stubby little bottles of cheap beer. We went to parties on other campsites or held parties of our own. Night after night, our tent rocked to the sounds of the Spin Doctors and the Red Hot Chili Peppers and a French rapper called MC Solaar. We only knew it was time to go to bed when the owners of the campsite switched our power off and plunged us into silence and darkness.

During quieter moments, me and Fi sat on our plastic chairs with our feet on our plastic table and listened to *Shooting Rubberbands at the Stars* by Edie Brickell & New Bohemians. In a sweet Texan drawl, Edie sang about friendship, love and the meaning of life. She was the perfect soundtrack to that carefree, wonderful summer.

One day, I stepped into the tent and found Fiona with a tangled ribbon of cassette tape in her hand. She looked worried. 'I'm really sorry,' she said. 'This crappy stereo ate your Nirvana tape.'

My Nirvana tape! *Nevermind*. My last precious link with the chip shop guy.

'Never mind,' I said, with a shrug. 'Have you got a pencil?'

Fiona rummaged through the clutter on the table, found one and passed it to me. Sinking into a chair, I poked the pointed end of the pencil into the centre of the cassette and began winding the crinkly ribbon back into place. I knew it was ruined but I wasn't upset. It's very hard to feel upset about anything when you eat ice-cream sandwiches and live in a tent with a friend who loves music as much as you do.

But life isn't always an ice-cream sandwich.

A few months later, Kurt Cobain died. Nirvana entered rock history and the songs I'd once loved now made me feel sad. I left my crackly copy of *Nevermind* in a drawer in my bedroom and went to Tunisia to work for a package holiday company. It was the start of a very up and down time for me. On the upside, I met a fun Scottish guy called Tom who introduced me to a noisy American rock band called Sugar. On the downside, I ate something that didn't agree with me and ended up in hospital on a drip. For a while, I lost over a stone in weight and all of my sense of humour.

As soon as I was well enough, I left Tunisia and went to Spain. On the downside, I couldn't eat anything other than boiled rice and vegetables. On the upside, my ears could still feast on anything! One day I was in a bar when I heard a song which made me want to dance with joy. It began with a blast of trumpets and was followed by a jazzy piano and a woman with a wonderful voice. She was singing a song all about ships and sailors and stormy seas. I listened right until the end and then I went to speak to the barman.

'What was that song you were just playing?' I asked.

'Wait.' The barman disappeared for a moment and then came back. 'It's called "Let's Wade in the Water" by Marlena Shaw. It was funky, huh?'

'*Really* funky,' I said, nodding. *Marlena Shaw.* I repeated the name a few times so that I wouldn't forget it. I needed to hear that record again.

When the job in Spain ended, I went back to France and worked on a hotel boat on the river Rhône. Every day, I made beds and cleaned bathrooms and looked out at passing riverbanks through tiny round portholes. On the downside, I hated it. On the upside, I had an hour or two to myself in a different place every day.

One afternoon, I went shopping in the city of Lyon and treated myself to a CD Walkman and a CD to go with it. I couldn't find anything by Marlena Shaw so I bought an album by a Britpop band called Elastica instead. As soon as I was out of the shop, I took the Walkman out of its box, filled it full of batteries and pushed the CD into position. Then I popped the earphones into my ears and pressed PLAY. A second later, I was blown away by a guitar as loud as a road drill. I'd never owned a CD player before and this level of private noise was new to me. Even though I scrubbed toilets and slept in a bunkbed, I walked back to my boat feeling like a millionaire

But in the end, not even a CD Walkman could keep me on that boat. One day, I woke up and decided I wanted to go home. I told the captain that I was quitting and that I'd like to leave as soon as possible and preferably that same day. I expected him to be annoyed but he wasn't. Instead, he wished me well and drove me to Avignon train station where I bought a ticket for the night train to Brussels. My plan was to visit a friend in the Belgian capital and then catch a train to the coast where I could board a ferry to take me home.

Just as I was about to get on my train, the captain handed me an envelope. 'This is for you, little one,' he said. 'Keep it safe.'

I took a peep inside and saw a fat wad of French

banknotes. Looking up in surprise, I said, 'What's this?'

'It's your share of all the tips we've had so far,' said the captain. 'I've been saving them for a rainy day.'

I stared at him, speechless.

'Don't miss your train,' he said. 'Otherwise you'll be coming back with me whether you like it or not.'

I didn't need telling twice. Quickly, I jumped on board and waved to this good captain until he was just a dot in the distance. His name was Lado and I'll never forget the kindness and patience he showed me that day. Or maybe he was just really relieved to be getting rid of me!

I didn't go home. All of a sudden, I had an envelope stuffed full of cash and a huge feeling of freedom. When daylight broke and my slow train from the south of France finally pulled into Brussels, I looked out at the heart of Europe and decided to stick around.

I soon found a job teaching English in a private language school and rented a room in a big shabby apartment close to the new European parliament. My flatmate was a Belgian woman, just the same age as me, called Sandrine. To begin with, Sandrine didn't speak a lot of English and I spoke even less French so we swapped polite smiles and kept out of each other's way. But before long, we were friends anyway. In that summer of 1995, the force that brought us together was an album:

No *Need to Argue* by The Cranberries.

Sandrine loved this album and so did I. She played it loudly and sang along, getting the words wrong every time. I taught her the right words and, in return, she taught me how to sing Blondie's 'Sunday Girl' in French.

After that we swapped more music. Sandrine made me listen to the greatest hits of a Belgian national hero called Jacques Brel. At first, I didn't like it. Jacques belonged in a world of black and white cinema and smoky music halls – he didn't belong in mine. But as I listened, I quickly began to understand that Jacques was no ordinary singer. He sang, he spoke, he purred and he chirruped. Sometimes, he blew words out of his mouth just as if he were blowing bubbles. I listened in amazement. Afterwards, Sandrine said, 'What do you think?'

'I really like it,' I said.

She played another CD by another Belgian singer called Arno. This time, I was less keen. When we got to the end of the CD, Sandrine asked me the same question. 'What do you think?'

'It's not my cup of tea,' I said.

My new friend looked confused. 'Why are you talking about tea?'

I tried again. 'I don't like it.'

'You're wrong,' she said, wrinkling her nose at my answer. 'But it's because you don't understand the words.'

Next, I made Sandrine listen to *Star* by Belly. She loved it so much that I gave her the CD. Then I played her my favourite album from the whole Britpop scene – *Elastica* by Elastica.

After only a couple of songs, Sandrine said, 'Stop! Who is this? She can't sing!'

'It's Justine Frischmann,' I said, outraged. 'She *can* sing but it's not just about her voice anyway. It's about *everything*!'

'*Non!*' Sandrine shook her head and lit a cigarette. 'It's awful. I don't like it.'

'Well, you're wrong,' I said, still outraged but starting to laugh. I pressed STOP, took my CD out of the stereo and replaced it with The Cranberries. The CD spun and a moment later, we were both singing along to the opening line of the first track. They were words which worked equally well in any language ...

Doo do-do-do ... Doo do-do-do ...

Me and Sandrine were mates and our disagreement over Arno and Elastica really didn't matter. There was *No Need to Argue*, after all.

CHAPTER FOURTEEN
A Random *Wow* Moment

I was nearly twenty-five and the most expensive thing I owned was a CD Walkman that skipped tracks unless I held it perfectly flat like a waiter holding a dinner plate. It wasn't a lot to show for a quarter of a century. I decided that it was time to start taking life a bit more seriously.

Packing up my things again, I waved goodbye to Brussels and took the Eurostar to London. I was going back to university to train as an English teacher. Actually, I already was one! I'd spent the past year explaining the difference between *much* and *many* to Belgian businessmen. Standing in a classroom full of teenagers and explaining why Shakespeare's jokes were funny seemed like the obvious thing for me to do next.

I found a cheap room in a big flat in north-west London and moved in. On the upside, my flatmates were easy to live with. There was Rosa from Barcelona, Robert from Berlin and Graham from Norwich. They were all friendly and polite and didn't leave their dirty dishes in the sink.

On the downside, I soon discovered that it wasn't just the four of us living in that flat. One morning, I went to get my breakfast and found Rosa guarding the door to the kitchen.

'I cannot let you go in there,' she said, firmly.

I looked at her, confused. 'Why?'

'Because there is a big rat eating biscuits in the cupboard. I'm sorry, I think they might be your biscuits. But don't worry. The people who kill the rats are on their way.'

Rats! Eating *my* biscuits! This was a new low.

Maybe I should have packed up my stuff again and moved straight out? If I'd had more money, I'm sure I would have done. But I was so short of cash that I stayed where I was. It turned out to be the best decision I have ever made.

Not long after I moved in, I heard music. Real *live* music. It wasn't being blasted into my ears through earphones and it wasn't coming out of the battered stereo in the corner of my room. It was music that was being made right *there and then*, somewhere in the flat. I opened my bedroom door and stuck my head into the hallway.

I could hear it a little clearer now. One of my flatmates was playing the guitar and filling the flat with a sad but beautiful tune that I felt sure I'd heard before. It wasn't an easy tune to play either. You couldn't strum this one. Whoever was playing was plucking the strings of the guitar like they were plucking a harp. Unable to stop myself, I followed the music down the hall until I came to a halt outside Graham's room. Then I stood still and listened. There was no mistaking it now. The tune escaping from under his door was 'Back to The Old House' by The Smiths. It was an old shoe shop favourite from the same album as 'Heaven Knows I'm Miserable Now'.

'Wow,' I whispered. I don't know whether I was whispering to Graham or to myself or simply to the stars – but I think the stars were listening anyway.

Smiling, I turned and tip-toed back to my room.

I didn't know it then but that random wow moment was the tiny little beginning of something very big. If I were making all of this up, I'd end this chapter now by telling you that Graham and I were married three months later.

I'm not going to do that because that would be silly romantic nonsense.

It wasn't three months. It was seven years.

CHAPTER FIFTEEN
The Sellotape Sisters

In the 1970s, I shared my mum's seven-inch singles and my dad's LPs. In the 1980s, I had cassette tapes of my own. In the 1990s, I moved on to CDs. In 2001, I turned thirty and fell in love with vinyl again. Life moves in strange circles sometimes.

There was one thing, though, which had stayed the same in all that time. Ever since that failed attempt at playing the keyboard when I was six, I'd only ever let myself *listen* to music. Anything else was a complete non-starter. That changed when I met Kirsty.

Graham and I were living in Cardiff and I was working in a high school. One day, I stuck my head into the staffroom in search of an extra pair of hands. The only person in there was Kirsty, a young student teacher. She was frowning over a huge stack of children's exercise books.

'Hi,' I said. 'I don't suppose you have a spare moment, do you?' It was an unfair question. We were in a school. Nobody ever had a spare moment.

Kirsty looked up from her books and nodded.

'Thanks,' I said, feeling grateful and guilty all at once. 'You're a lifesaver!'

We walked to my classroom. When we got there, I pointed to a huge pile of posters and bright pink paper and said, 'I need help turning all of this into a wall display.'

Kirsty nodded again, picked up the staple-gun and climbed on to a chair. I did the same and, for a while, we stood on our tiptoes and stapled pink paper to the wall in a busy silence. Then, I said, 'So how are you finding it here?'

'Yeah, I like it – it's good.' Kirsty fired another staple into our new bright pink backdrop.

'Are your classes OK?'

'Yeah. They're good, thanks.'

I smiled and then scratched my head. Some people talk too much. Kirsty clearly wasn't one of them.

We kept on working and the silence stretched out between us. The only noises were the TICK TICK TICK of the classroom clock and the BANG BANG BANG of the staple gun.

Maybe I'm really scary, I thought. A second thought struck me and I frowned. *Maybe it's because I'm getting old and I'm asking really boring questions?* I tried again. 'So ... um ... so do you like music?'

It was like I'd said a secret password! Kirsty's face lit up. 'Oh my god, yeah,' she said. 'I *love* music!'

I breathed a sigh of relief and grinned. 'So what kind of thing do you like?'

Kirsty lowered her staple gun and looked thoughtful. A moment later, she said, 'Curtis Stigers.'

'*Curtis Stigers?*' I was so surprised I nearly toppled off my chair.

'Yeah,' said Kirsty, a big grin spreading across her face. 'I've got all his albums and I'm also the proud owner of a mug with his face on it.'

My mouth opened but I couldn't think of a single word to say! Curtis Stigers was a name I hadn't heard since the very early nineties. The only song of his that I could name was a power ballad called 'I Wonder Why'. It was the kind of thing that you might hear playing in the middle of the night on a radio station called Swoon FM.

'Don't look at me like that,' said Kirsty, laughing. 'I play the saxophone and Curtis is actually a great saxophone player! I'm telling you – he's a genius, he really is.'

'I believe you,' I said. 'I just ... I just wasn't expecting such an unusual answer.'

Kirsty turned red but kept on laughing. 'I like a lot of other stuff too,' she said. 'But you asked me an interesting question and I wanted to give you a *truly* interesting answer.'

For a moment, all I could do was stare at Kirsty as I turned this piece of wisdom over in my mind. Then

I smiled and gave her a nod of respect. 'You *truly* did,' I said.

Time ticked on and Kirsty got a job in my school as an English teacher. I was delighted. In between marking books and planning lessons and punching staples into the walls, we talked about music. I learned that Kirsty didn't just love Curtis Stigers. She was also a massive fan of Super Furry Animals and a very strange band called David Devant and His Spirit Wife. One day, I told her that Graham and I were going to Bristol at the weekend to check out the record shops. I asked her if she'd like to come with us.

Kirsty's face lit up but then, almost instantly, it fell again. 'Oh hang on,' she said. 'My record deck is in north Wales with my mum. I don't actually listen to vinyl anymore.'

'Well, it's just a fun day out,' I said. 'It's up to you.'

Kirsty's face lit up again. 'I could always look at the CDs,' she said.

And so it was settled. The following Saturday, we all caught the train to Bristol and went in search of record shops. Graham had done his research. Armed with a map and a notepad, he led us towards the bus station and down some steps into a concrete underpass. It looked like the worst place in the world to put a shop. In fact, it looked like the worst place in the world to put anything! But there was no chance that we had taken a wrong turning because we heard the shop before we saw it. The music booming through the underpass was so loud that I had to force myself not to turn around and go somewhere else.

'THIS BETTER BE WORTH IT!' I shouted to Graham.

'IT WILL BE,' he shouted back, his eyes filled with excitement. 'I LOOKED ON THE INTERNET AND EVERYONE RECKONS THAT REPLAY RECORDS IS THE BEST PLACE TO START.' He looked at Kirsty and grinned. 'HOW ARE YOU ENJOYING BRISTOL SO FAR?'

Kirsty stuck her thumb up. 'I THINK YOU ARE SHOWING ME ALL THE BEST BITS,' she bellowed.

We pushed open the shop door and went in.

After the gloom of the underpass, the shop seemed dazzling. I blinked and let my eyes adjust to the strip lighting. What I saw next made me smile. There were records everywhere! Of course there were – we were in a record shop! But even though I'd been in hundreds of record shops, the thrill of finding a new one was still as strong as ever! For a second, I was back in the record department of Woolworths in Ipswich in 1981. There were new records shrink-wrapped in plastic. There were old records with scuffed sleeves. There were LPs and there were singles. But I couldn't see any CDs. I cast a worried glance at Kirsty and hoped she wouldn't be bored. She didn't *look* bored. She was gazing around with wide eyes and seemed just as excited as me and Graham.

We split up and started flicking through the racks of vinyl. It was odd but the music *inside* the shop didn't seem as loud as it had outside in the underpass. Maybe it was because our eyes were now busier than our ears? I don't know why but I started with the albums grouped under the letter S. S was as good a place to start as any. It stood for The Smiths and The Stone Roses and ... and *Marlena Shaw*!

A bell rang in my head. I grabbed the record out of the rack and Marlena Shaw stared back at me sternly from the sleeve. It was just as if she were saying, 'You took your time, Hayley!'

I flipped the record over in my hands. Track 4 on Side A was a song called 'Let's Wade in the Water'. A memory of a bar in Spain flashed into my head.

'Oh my god,' I said. 'I've just found the funkiest record in the whole world!'

'So have I,' said Graham. He held up an LP record in a plain white sleeve. It looked like a dodgy bootleg. 'This is called *Groove Master Classics*. There's some great stuff on here.'

Just then, Kirsty appeared. She was holding a stack of LPs and had a huge smile on her face. 'I *love* this place,' she said. 'I've already found a ton of records I want.'

'But your record player is in north Wales with your mum,' I said, laughing.

Kirsty shrugged and looked happier than ever. 'I'll just have to buy a new one,' she said.

In fact, she bought two. They were shining silver DJ decks and they were beautiful. They pulled me around to Kirsty's flat like a magnet. Together, we learned how to use both turntables at once and how to fade one record into the next. We learned how to count the beats of a song and how to match them perfectly with the beats of another. Most importantly, we learned that nothing sounded finer on those decks than nonstop funk and soul music. Soon, we were making DJ playlists ...

1. 'Rock Steady' – Aretha Franklin
2. 'We Can Work It Out' – Stevie Wonder
3. 'Spooky' – Dusty Springfield
4. 'If You Want Me to Stay' – Sly and The Family Stone
5. 'I'm a Man' – Spencer Davis Group
6. 'Let's Wade in the Water' – Marlena Shaw

'We're getting good at this,' said Kirsty, one day. 'We should call ourselves The Staple Gun Sisters and become world famous DJs.'

I laughed. '*Staple Gun?*' I'm not sure. Does that sound a bit violent?'

'Yeah, maybe.' Suddenly, Kirsty clicked her fingers. 'I know! How about The Sellotape Sisters?'

'Perfect,' I said. 'Let's get famous.'

Our first ever gig was right near Cardiff Castle in a trendy little hangout called Café Bar Europa. When we arrived, we found two bald blokes already sitting behind the record decks.

'I'm really sorry,' said the bar manager. 'I got the dates wrong and made a double booking. Maybe you guys can work something out together and play half the night each?'

Kirsty and I quickly agreed but the other two DJs were less keen. One of them waved his hand at the busy bar. 'We've got all these people to think about. We can't just let a couple of girls come in here and play any old rubbish.'

'We're not going to play *any old rubbish*,' I said, my cheeks suddenly burning.

'Oh yeah?' The two guys were now sneering at the silver record boxes that Kirsty and I had put down at our feet. 'What have you got in there? Steps? S Club 7?'

'Aretha Franklin,' said Kirsty. 'She's not rubbish. Neither is Stevie Wonder or Candi Staton.'

I smiled. These two clowns clearly didn't know who they were dealing with.

There was a short pause and then they looked at each other and sighed. 'OK, OK,' one of them said. 'No need to get your knickers in a knot. You two can take over now and we'll be back in ninety minutes to pick up the pieces.'

Kirsty and I nodded wordlessly. Ninety minutes was better than nothing.

'You do *know* how to use a record deck, don't you?' he added, suddenly looking worried. 'We don't want to come back and find that you've broken anything.'

'Yeah, and don't try anything clever,' said his mate. 'As if you could!' With that, they laughed and went.

We didn't break anything. And we didn't try anything clever. We just played our records and had the best time ever! When the two clowns came back, they found a bar full of happy people and a delighted bar manager who told them how well we had done. They looked at us in surprise and then gave us grudging nods of respect. 'You've done well for a couple of birds,' they said.

After that, we played our records in bars and clubs all over Cardiff. Every gig was a total joy. Once, we took our records on the train and played a short set in a packed trendy bar in north-west London. That was on the day that Graham and I got married. For one hour, I was the DJ at my own wedding!

But there was one other very special gig that we played at. It wasn't in any trendy bar or club – it was in the school where Kirsty and I worked. Year 11 were having a disco and we'd been asked to DJ. We were nervous! As the hall filled up with excited students, Kirsty and I looked at each other and a single question flashed between us:

Would these fifteen-year-olds want to
dance to Dusty Springfield?

I looked down at our four newest records. They were all 12 inch remixes.

'Crazy in Love' – Beyoncé
'Toxic' – Britney Spears
'Hey Ya!' – Outkast
'Seven Nation Army' – The White Stripes

'Do you think we're going to get away with this?' I said.

Kirsty nodded. 'If the worst comes to the worst, we can always play those four on repeat for two hours.'

We started with Beyoncé. The kids went mad and started jumping up and down. Clearly, they weren't going to waste any time getting warmed up. They were here to enjoy every single second. As that record was coming to an end, we mixed it with Outkast. As soon as the vocals kicked in, the kids cheered. This was going well. *But for how long?*

Kirsty pulled an album out of its sleeve. 'Let's see how they get on with Aretha Franklin,' she said. Listening through one ear of her headphones, she gently put the record needle down on the black vinyl and then pushed another button to get it spinning. There was no overlap this time. Outkast ended and the opening riff of 'Respect' rang out around the school hall.

The cheer that went up was the loudest so far. Kirsty and I beamed at each other in relief. For a moment, we just stood and watched as two hundred teenagers bounced up and down and sang along to a feminist anthem. It was a happy sight.

I took another album out of its sleeve. 'I'm going to mix this in,' I said. 'Hopefully, they'll just keep on dancing.'

I put the needle on the record and then reached over to the control box and slid a fader switch. Then I nudged up the volume and held my breath.

Aretha was still singing but now there was another track playing in the background. The dancing in the hall didn't stop. It didn't even slow down. I moved the fader a little further. Aretha vanished into the mix and another woman started to sing. Her song was all about ships and sailors and stormy seas and it was so joyous that it made me want to jump off the stage and start dancing with the kids. It made me feel glad to be alive.

'They love it,' said Kirsty, laughing. 'They absolutely love it.'

Again, we stood and watched in happy amazement at the scene in front of us.

And then I spotted something. A boy called Tim had made his way over to us and was trying to speak to me. I knelt down on the edge of the stage so I could hear what he was saying.

Through cupped hands, he shouted again. 'WHAT IS THIS SONG?'

I cupped my own hands and shouted back. '"LET'S WADE IN THE WATER". IT'S BY MARLENA SHAW.'

Tim pointed at his ear and frowned.

'WAIT,' I said. Reaching around into my bag, I pulled out a pen and a post-it note and scribbled it down.

Tim looked at the little slip of paper and nodded and put it carefully into the pocket of his jeans. Then he said, 'I'VE NEVER EVEN HEARD OF IT. IS IT NEW?'

'NOT EXACTLY,' I said, 'BUT IT'S NEW TO YOU.'

Tim grinned and held his thumb up. 'IT'S THE COOLEST TRACK EVER,' he said.

I wanted to hug him. Instead, I glanced over my shoulder to share this moment with my friend but she had her headphones on and was lost in music. I turned around again to speak to Tim but he was already back in the crowd and jumping up and down with his mates. They were all happily freaking out to a song that they were hearing for the very first time in their lives.

I smiled. These kids were open to new things. The future was definitely alright.

CHAPTER SIXTEEN

So What Does
It All Mean?

I still have lots of records – and tapes and CDs – but I don't DJ anymore. I write books instead and music creeps into everything I write. I hope it always will.

But what does any of it mean? Why do I hear magic when Tanya Donelly picks up a guitar and lets off some steam? Why do I turn up the volume when Kurt Cobain or Laura Marling mutters into a microphone? Why does a song called 'Let's Wade in The Water' fill me with the deepest joy? And how on earth can a noisy din by Lawnmower Deth do exactly the same thing?

There are no quick answers to any of these questions. That's why I've written this book. Music is a strange and magical thing. What sounds amazing to one person might sound awful to another. Not everything I like is cheerful, well known or even easy to listen to. But one thing I *do* know is that there's nothing quite like the buzz of falling in love with one of these songs and then finding someone else who loves it too. It reminds me of something my flatmate Sandrine once said to me in Brussels.

'You are so funny,' she said. 'You love pop music so much that I think you would choose your friends by the CDs they listen to.'

When she said this, I burst out laughing. I'm still laughing now.

Making friends through music. Is there any better way?

One last thing.

Writing a book is a bit like doing a huge jigsaw puzzle. Sometimes there are a few pieces which won't fit in. I can't finish this book without mentioning ...

My dad who gave me The Beatles and The Beach Boys and so much more.

My cousin Melanie who took me to see Michael Jackson at Wembley Stadium in 1987.

Fiona from Felixstowe (Noz's sister) who really deserves a whole book of her own.

Tara who was with me and Lynda in Aberystwyth, and who knows every word to the rap in the 12-inch remix of Soft Cell's 'Bedsitter'. As do I.

My friend Tracey who was with me in Belgium when we saw Paul Weller and M People and Urban Species and MC Solaar. And as well as that, she let me sleep on her sofa in Brussels for about eight weeks.

To these people, I must quote another band I liked very much when everything I heard came in square paper sleeves and cost 50p from Woolworths or Boots ...

Thank you for the music.

CONGRATULATIONS ON COMPLETING A 2019 QUICK READ.

The Quick Reads project, with bite-sized books, is designed to get readers back into the swing of reading, and reading for pleasure. So we sincerely hope you enjoyed this book.

Got an opinion?

Your feedback can make this project better. Now you've read one of the Quick Reads series visit www.readingwalcs.org.uk or Twitter @quickreads2019 to post your feedback.

→ Why did you choose this book?

→ What did you like about it?

→ What do you think of the Quick Reads series?

→ Which Quick Reads would you like to see in the future?

WHAT NEXT?

Now that you've finished one Quick Read – got time for another? Look out for the other title in the 2019 Quick Reads series – *Reset Your Goals* by Jos Andrews.

Don't worry about failures – worry about the chances you miss when you don't even try. Sportsmen and women talk honestly about dealing with success and disappointment. The common message is, 'I might get knocked down but I get up again. Setbacks are challenges but they don't defeat me.' In the words of Wales' Olympic gold medallist:

'If it's to be, it's up to me.'

Lynn Davies

Nine top sporting personalities talk frankly about their personal highs and lows. Read their inspirational stories for just £1!

rily.co.uk

MORE ABOUT QUICK READS

Quick Reads started in 2006 and are a series of short books by bestselling authors and celebrities. With no more than 128 pages, they are designed to encourage adults who do not read often, or find reading difficult, to discover the joy of books.

In Wales the project is also known as Quick Reads, or Stori Sydyn in Welsh. The scheme is coordinated by the Welsh Books Council, supported by the Welsh Government and aims to encourage people to look afresh at reading through entertaining short books. The Quick Reads initiative is designed specifically for people who have either lost the reading habit or who wish to improve their skills and confidence around reading.

The Quick Read books are also used as a resource for adult literacy teaching and have been used in secondary schools, colleges, community centres, libraries, prisons and workplaces across the country. They have also been used in hospitals, stroke recovery units, dyslexia centres, care homes, family learning groups, pre-schools, organisations working with homeless people and traveller communities, and Army and RAF bases.

In a survey covering 50,000 new readers in 2010, 98% said that:

"Quick Reads had made a positive impact on their lives".

Hayley Long

Hayley was born in Ipswich and grew up by the sea in Felixstow. She had a lot of different jobs before she started writing books. Amongst other things, she sold shoes, folded sweaters, pulled pints, cleaned tents, guided people through a Tunisian *souk*, did vague things in various offices, and taught English in Brussels, London, Cardiff and Norwich! But, for now, she is devoted exclusively to reading and writing.

Hayley is already a multi-award winning author. Her latest novel *The Nearest Faraway Place* won the prestigious 2018 Tir na n-Og literary award. This prize, organised by the Welsh Books Council, promotes English-language children's books with an authentic Welsh background. Hayley also won the Mal Peet Children's Award when this novel was also named the winner of the children's category in the 2017 East Anglian Book Awards.

Her first novel for teens was *Lottie Biggs is Not Mad*. This was awarded the White Raven Award for exceptional and innovative books for children by the International Youth Library in Munich. Since then, she has had a lot more books published, been translated into more than fifteen languages and been shortlisted for a Costa book award – twice!! Hayley was also shortlisted for the Queen of Teen Awards.

Hayley currently lives in Norwich with her husband and her official website is www.hayleylong.org

rily.co.uk